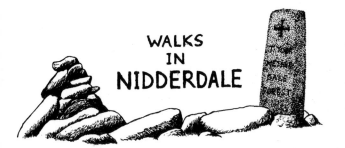

WALKS
IN
NIDDERDALE

HILLSIDE GUIDES by PAUL HANNON

- **1983** **THE WESTMORLAND WAY**
  98 miles from Appleby to Arnside
- **1984** **THE FURNESS WAY**
  75 miles from Arnside to Ravenglass
- **1985** **THE CUMBERLAND WAY**
  80 miles from Ravenglass <u>to</u> Appleby

THE YORKSHIRE DALES

~~ National Park Boundary

N ↑

Keld · SWALEDALE · Reeth

Sedbergh

WESTERN DALES

Hawes · WENSLEYDALE · Aysgarth

Ingleton

Buckden

WHARFEDALE

Horton

Ramsgill

NIDDERDALE

Pateley Bridge

Settle · Malham · CRAVEN DALES · Grassington

Gargrave

Skipton

- **1985** **WALKS IN WHARFEDALE**
  18 circular walks
- **1985** **WALKS IN NIDDERDALE**
  18 circular walks
- **1986** **WALKS IN THE CRAVEN DALES**
  16 circular walks

WALKS
IN
NIDDERDALE

by

Paul Hannon

HILLSIDE  PUBLICATIONS

HILLSIDE PUBLICATIONS
11 Nessfield Grove
Exley Head
Keighley
West Yorkshire
BD22 6NU

First published 1985
2nd impression 1986

for Sarah

Cover illustration: Scar House and Angram Reservoirs
and Great Whernside from Carle Side Quarry
Page 1 : Summit of South Haw
(both from Walk 16)

ISBN 0 9509212 4 6

Printed in Great Britain by
Carnmor Print and Design
95/97 London Road
Preston
Lancashire
PR1 4BA

INTRODUCTION

Although far from being the least attractive of the Yorkshire Dales, Nidderdale is probably the least known. The main reason for this seems clear: by virtue of it's exclusion from the National Park, it is also automatically excluded from the itinerary of most visitors. The twin 'gateways' of Harrogate and Knaresborough certainly receive their share of attention but the equally accessible and far more 'glamorous' valleys of the Wharfe and the Ure are more likely to be the next stop. All this leaves Nidderdale free from congestion and leaves the rambler 'free' to roam, often in solitude, over the 18 walks described in this guide.

The stretch of the valley of the Nidd with which this guide deals is from the head of the dale down to the major river crossing at Summerbridge. Below here, Nidderdale is more commonly referred to as the Nidd Valley, and the scenery becomes tamer. Initially this guide was intended to include the lower valley, but such a wealth of enjoyable walks was discovered that the lower boundary of the area continually crept up-dale, leaving us with the best that Nidderdale has to offer.

Despite it's relative solitude, Nidderdale is renowned far and wide for several features, notably the vastly differing natural attractions of Brimham Rocks and How Stean Gorge. Following close behind are the holes of Goyden Pot and Manchester Hole, which swallow the Nidd in it's early stages. Further still up the dale are the reservoirs of Scar House and Angram, in an extremely bleak setting overshadowed by the highest fells. Add to this Gouthwaite Reservoir, Yorke's Folly and Guise Cliff, and sleepy, unspoilt villages like Ramsgill and Wath, and we are at last scratching the surface. Aside from the natural rockscapes and the man-made lakes, Nidderdale boasts two other outstanding aspects — namely trees and heather. The valley is nothing short of lavished with attractive woodland, whilst above the fields but below the fell-tops are marvellous expanses of moorland, particularly on the eastern side of the dale.

The 18 walks in this guide vary in length from 3 to 9 miles, and the terrain varies equally from modest riverside strolls to rather more strenuous fell-walks. All of the walks are circular and with an average distance of 5½ miles they are ideally suited for half-day rambles. Each walk has it's own chapter, consisting of an immediate impression' diagram, detailed narrative and strip-map, and notes and illustrations of places of interest.

Almost all of the miles covered are on public rights-of-way, those which are not are within water-board grounds at the dale-head, or in high altitude open country. A mention must be made of the access regulations pertaining to the Yorkshire Water Authority land. The environs of Scar House Reservoir and the road from Lofthouse thereto are open to the public, subject to various restrictions. These are detailed at the start of the road, where a fee must also be paid by motorists. The main points are a) a limit of 150 vehicles in the grounds, and b) the road is closed at the end of the day. For a payment of 50p (in 1985) the head of the valley is opened up and three of our walks take advantage of this facility.

Three final comments before we pull on our boots: 1) the omission-maybe surprisingly- of Nidderdale's highest fell and only 2000-footer, Great Whernside, is simply due to it rating as a little more than a half-day ramble.

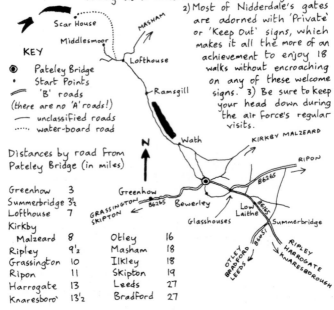

2) Most of Nidderdale's gates are adorned with 'Private' or 'Keep Out' signs, which makes it all the more of an achievement to enjoy 18 walks without encroaching on any of these welcome signs. 3) Be sure to keep your head down during the air force's regular visits.

Scar House
Middlesmoor
MASHAM

KEY

◉ Pateley Bridge
• Start Points
⚊ 'B' roads
(there are no 'A' roads!)
— unclassified roads
······ water-board road

Lofthouse

Ramsgill

Wath
KIRKBY MALZEARD
RIPON
B6265
Greenhow
GRASSINGTON/SKIPTON ← B6265 Bewerley
Glasshouses
Low Laithe
Summerbridge
B6451
B6165
OTLEY/BRADFORD/LEEDS
RIPLEY
HARROGATE
KNARESBOROUGH

N

Distances by road from Pateley Bridge (in miles)

Greenhow	3		
Summerbridge	3½		
Lofthouse	7		
Kirkby Malzeard	8	Otley	16
Ripley	9½	Masham	18
Grassington	10	Ilkley	18
Ripon	11	Skipton	19
Harrogate	13	Leeds	27
Knaresboro'	13½	Bradford	27

6

FACILITIES AT STARTING POINTS AND VILLAGES VISITED

	Accommodation	Inn	Car Park	Bus service	Post Office	Shop	Toilets
Bewerley	-	-	-	-	-	-	-
Dacre Banks	✓	✓	✓	✓	-	✓	✓
Glasshouses	✓	✓	-	✓	✓	✓	✓
Greenhow	✓	✓	-	✓	✓	-	-
Lofthouse	✓	✓	✓	-	✓	-	✓
Low Laithe	-	✓	-	✓	-	✓	-
Middlesmoor	-	✓	✓	-	✓	-	✓
Pateley Bridge	✓	✓	✓	✓	✓	✓	✓
Ramsgill	✓	✓	-	-	-	-	-
Scar House	-	-	✓	-	-	-	✓
Summerbridge	✓	✓	✓	✓	✓	✓	-
Wath	✓	✓	✓	-	-	-	-

The above includes all known details, and, particularly with
accommodation, omissions/changes may occur. This first facility
is barely adequate above Pateley Bridge: bed and breakfasts are
a rarity outside of the hotels. The obvious base, certainly
for the car-owner, is Pateley Bridge. The only Youth Hostel
is at Dacre Banks, on the very edge of this guide's area. The
recent closure of Longside House between Ramsgill and Lofthouse,
a magnificently-sited hostel, was a veritable tragedy. Camping can
be had at Pateley Bridge and Studfold, near Lofthouse. Above
indication of a car-park or toilet means other than hotel or
inn facilities; a lay-by at least (for parking, not the latter).
Pateley's early-closing is on Thursday, Harrogate's Wednesday,
while Knaresborough's is Thursday, with market-day Wednesday.

ORDNANCE SURVEY MAPS

The strip-maps illustrating each walk should guide one safely around, but will show nothing of the surrounding countryside: the simple remedy is an Ordnance Survey map, as follows:-

1:50,000 metric scale
sheet 99: Northallerton and Ripon
sheet 98: Wensleydale and Wharfedale
(the latter serves only walks 5 and 10)

1 inch to the mile
sheet 90: Wensleydale
sheet 91: Ripon

PUBLIC TRANSPORT

The nearest railway stations are at Harrogate and at Knaresborough. Of these, Harrogate is more accessible, and it is from here that the buses make their way up the valley. Nidderdale's bus services are not too complicated to understand, as there is really only one of any use in our area. Passing through Dacre Banks, the main valley road is followed to Pateley Bridge: this is now the terminus of the service that until recently ran all the way up to Middlesmoor. The only other services are occasional ones that link Pateley Bridge with Greenhow and Brimham Rocks.

DRINKING IN NIDDERDALE

Like the River Nidd itself, traditional beer does not exactly flow freely in the upper valley, but is readily available below Pateley Bridge. Of the following breweries supplying the real thing, only the first two mentioned (notably the only two independent concerns) can be totally relied upon in their rare Nidderdale showings.

Timothy Taylor, Keighley   Sam Smith, Tadcaster
John Smith, Tadcaster   Tetley, Leeds
Theakston, Masham and Carlisle
and lastly, Younger, Edinburgh

8

SOME USEFUL ADDRESSES

Ramblers' Association
    1/5 Wandsworth Road, London SW8 2LJ
        Tel. 01-582 6878

Youth Hostels Association
    Trevelyan House, St.Albans, Herts. AL1 2DY
        Tel. 0727-55215
    Regional Office:
      96 Main Street, Bingley, W.Yorkshire BD16 2JH
        Tel. Bradford (0274) 567697

Yorkshire and Humberside Tourist Board
    312 Tadcaster Road, York YO2 2HF
        Tel. 0904-707961

West Yorkshire Road Car Company
    P.O. Box 24, East Parade,
    Harrogate, North Yorkshire HG1 5LS
        Tel. 0423-66061

The National Trust
    36 Queen Anne's Gate, London SW1H 9AS
        Tel. 01-222 9251
    Membership: P.O. Box 30, Beckenham,
          Kent BR3 4TL

Tourist Information Centre (open all year)
    Royal Baths Assembly Rooms, Crescent Rd,
    Harrogate, North Yorkshire
        Tel. 0423-65912

Campaign for Real Ale
    34 Alma Road, St.Albans, Herts. AL1 3BW

THE WALKS

Listed below are the 18 walks described, the walk number being the Key to easy location in the guide

Walks in Nidderdale

outline map showing the starting
points and the routes of the walks

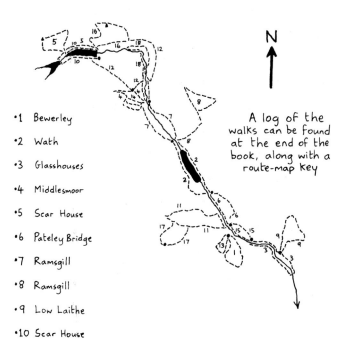

N

A log of the
walks can be found
at the end of the
book, along with a
route-map key

- 1 Bewerley
- 2 Wath
- 3 Glasshouses
- 4 Middlesmoor
- 5 Scar House
- 6 Pateley Bridge
- 7 Ramsgill
- 8 Ramsgill
- 9 Low Laithe
- 10 Scar House
- 11 Pateley Bridge
- 12 Middlesmoor
- 13 Bewerley
- 14 Lofthouse
- 15 Pateley Bridge
- 16 Scar House
- 17 Greenhow
- 18 Lofthouse

WALK 1

4 miles

YORKE'S FOLLY AND GUISECLIFF WOOD

from Bewerley

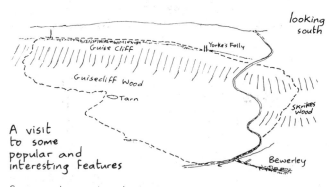

looking south

Guise Cliff

Yorke's Folly

Guisecliff Wood

Tarn

Skrikes Wood

Bewerley

A visit
to some
popular and
interesting features

Bewerley has adequate
roadside parking alongside or near the green

THE WALK

Leave Bewerley along the lane through the village away from Pateley Bridge, past Bewerley Grange Chapel to turn right at the second junction, just across a bridge. At the first bend take a stile on the right, heading straight up the large field to a stile admitting to Skrikes Wood. A partly-paved way leads out of the top of the wood and a good track weaves through bracken, past an old quarry and up to a stile.

A fence accompanies the track up onto a moor-road, but straight across it our track heads freely through the heather to the unmistakeable twin towers of Yorke's Folly. Just beyond, a wall is crossed, and again a good path shadows it between moor and woods. After a stile in a fence the exposed top of Guise Cliff is attained, and the path runs along virtually the entire length, giving superlative views over the vertical drop to the extensive woods below.

On reaching the very prominent T.V. mast,

another stile is crossed, then the perimeter of the confines of the mast is skirted to a gate just beyond. Pass through and down to another gate from where a path re-appears to bend round to the left, entering Guisecliff Wood as a wide track. After a number of bends and undulations the track swings sharp right to drop a little more steeply: just after this take a path branching left to visit the deeply-inurned Guisecliff Tarn, before returning us back onto the main track.

Our track eventually leaves the wood by a gate, crossing the right side of a field to join a farm-track whose downhill curve leads us to the farm of Baylis Gap. Keep left of all the buildings, to a gate from where a pleasant level track heads away. From a gate in the field-corner a rather sketchy track again heads away in a straight line, through two gateways, past a solitary tree and out onto a lane. Turn left to Turner Bridge, which is crossed to re-enter Bewerley village.

Yorke's Folly

The small village of Bewerley, near neighbour of Pateley Bridge, contains a host of attractive cottages nestling in peace. Mentioned in the Domesday Book, Bewerley is a world apart from it's big brother across the river. The area was given to the monks of Fountains Abbey, who erected a grange here. The Grange Chapel, dating from the end of the 15th century, has been well restored in modern times: it stands in charming grounds in the village centre.

The spacious 'park' is used for the dale's big annual event, the Pateley Show.

The magnificent rock architecture of Guise Cliff forms a splendid sight from below, but from above as on this walk, the spectacle is still greater. Children and vertigo sufferers should NOT be near the edge. The blanket of woodland below is so complete that it hides the still waters of the oval tarn in it's midst.

N

PATELEY BRIDGE

Bewerley

Chapel

GREENHOW

Raven's Gill

Turner Bridge

GLASSHOUSES

Baylis Gap

Skrikes Wood

old quarry

ROAD

HEBDEN

Yorke's Folly

Guisecliff Tarn

Guisecliff Wood

Guise Cliff

TV mast

Small but pleasant, Skrikes Wood has been designated a Nature Reserve, chiefly for it's varieties of bird-life.

From the author's brief acquaintance with Baylis Gap, it can be assumed that muddy feet are a fairly safe bet.

Though not included in the text, a detour to Crocodile Rock is recommended: essential, even, for Reg Dwight fans. It adds on a mere 10 minutes

Highly prominent from a host of locations, Yorke's Folly is a 'firm favourite' in the Nidderdale scene. Built 200 years ago by a member of the Yorke family in order to provide local employment, and also to resemble a Rhineland ruin. Two tall towers remain, the largest having succumbed to a severe storm in 1893.

2

WALK 2

7 miles

GOUTHWAITE RESERVOIR

from Wath

A simple circuit of the reservoir - be sure to take your binoculars

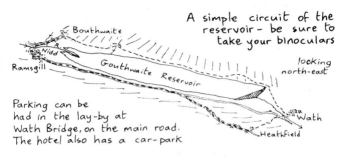

!looking north-east

Parking can be had in the lay-by at Wath Bridge, on the main road. The hotel also has a car-park

THE WALK

From Wath Bridge take the stile on the village side and follow the river upstream. After a second stile the path crosses the centre of a field to enter trees, with the increasing roar of the water leaving Gouthwaite's hidden dam. A stile and a gate lead to a locked gate at the top-corner of the dam. Our path takes a gateway opposite to rise across two fields to join a wide track: the geography of this walk can be well appraised from our early vantage point.

Following this track to the left, it soon descends almost to the very shore of the reservoir. All that separates us is the green line of the old railway track, sadly the property of the water board. Our own track continues mostly parallel with the line for the entire length of Gouthwaite, the only deviation being through the attractive farm grouping at Covelle Houses. Beyond the farm the track acquires a more solid base before reaching Bouthwaite at the head of the reservoir. A left turn at this crossroads of lanes leads to Nidd Bridge on the edge of Ramsgill village.

After a sojourn on the green, continue south on the road out of the village. Gouthwaite Reservoir soon returns to our side and the road now clings to it's shore for two winding miles, until

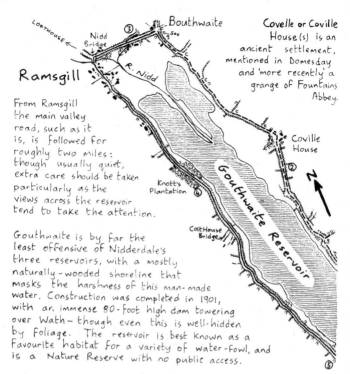

Bouthwaite

← LOFTHOUSE ←

Nidd Bridge

Ramsgill

R. Nidd

Covelle or Coville House(s) is an ancient settlement, mentioned in Domesday and 'more recently' a grange of Fountains Abbey.

Coville House

N

Gouthwaite Reservoir

Knott's Plantation

ColtHouse Bridge

From Ramsgill the main valley road, such as it is, is followed for roughly two miles: though usually quiet, extra care should be taken particularly as the views across the reservoir tend to take the attention.

Gouthwaite is by far the least offensive of Nidderdale's three reservoirs, with a mostly naturally-wooded shoreline that masks the harshness of this man-made water. Construction was completed in 1901, with an immense 80-foot high dam towering over Wath — though even this is well-hidden by foliage. The reservoir is best known as a favourite habitat for a variety of water-fowl, and is a Nature Reserve with no public access.

THE WALK continued

After passing the striking frontage of the 'new' Gouthwaite Hall, a narrow, winding strip of tarmac leaves the road through a cattle-grid. Not sign-posted and resembling a private drive, this traffic-free lane rises steeply, passing through a thick wood before levelling out to arrive at the scattered group of dwellings at Heathfield.

As the lane slowly descends, opt for the drive down to the left to Spring Hill Farm, going straight across the yard to a gate at the far side. Directly across the field is a stile: leave it by descending half-left across two large fields, then crossing straight over two smaller fields (stiles/gates provided) to drop down to the road, exactly opposite the lay-by at Wath Bridge.

Gouthwaite Reservoir from Colthouse Bridge

Wath is a tiny, unspoilt village in a fine wooded setting: it is a desperate shame that there are no rights-of-way by which to explore the hills and becks of it's hinterland. Though widened almost a century ago, Wath Bridge is still small enough to recall the days when it is thought the monks of Fountains Abbey used it as a packhorse bridge. The attractive inn stands close by the site of Wath's railway station on the Nidd Valley Light Railway.

The railway's course hugs the shore of the reservoir, and for the most part our route runs close, often parallel. There being no access to the reservoir grounds we are unable to make use of it, though it seems some may be too tempted by the inviting green line.

The hamlet of Heathfield is an ancient settlement once used by the ubiquitous Yorke family for smelting ore from their mines.

Gouthwaite Reservoir

Gouthwaite Hall ↗

This was built in 1901 as a replacement for the original hall which was drowned by the reservoir. Parts of the hall have been retained in this new building.

→ WATH

West Wood

N

⑥

Spring Hill

Heathfield

→ PATELEY BRIDGE

River Nidd

RAMSGILL ←

Wath

redundant bus shelter

↘ PATELEY BRIDGE

There are fine views over the reservoir early on the climb to Heathfield

WALK 3

THE BANKS OF THE NIDD

6 miles

from Glasshouses

Very easy walking, using the river to link the mid-valley villages

Glasshouses

looking
north-east

Low Laithe

River Nidd

Summerbridge

Dacre Banks

Park alongside the
sloping green in the
village centre

THE WALK

From the village green take the lane down towards the river, but before reaching the bridge enter the large mill-yard on the left, turning right immediately after the main building. Passing down the side of it a track descends towards the river. Our way now clings to the riverbank, through several stiles, past the remains of the old viaduct, and then past a wooden footbridge. After a sheltering canopy of trees a tributary beck is met: here leave the river to accompany the beck up to a tiny footbridge. Cross it and continue up the field to emerge onto the main valley road. A right turn leads into the village of Low Laithe.

Remain on this road, with a pavement all the way, through Low Laithe and on to the next village of Summerbridge. Turn right at the road junction by the inn to drop down to bridge the river, with it's companion village of Dacre Banks just ahead. Our route does not however enter the village proper, but takes a fenced path on the right, skirting the boundary of the extensive timber yard.

Over a tiny footbridge we rejoin the river in a large meadow, at the far end using a stile to join a wide track. Turn right along it, crossing the former railway line and soon returning to run parallel with the course of the old line. Soon a gate gains entry into a wooded area, and after ignoring a branch left, take

Glasshouses

the right-hand option at an obvious fork. We are now on the exact line of the old railway, but after only a short distance fork right again, on a path descending to the very edge of the river.

From here on we again cling to the riverbank to lead us all the way back to the singularly unglamorous Glasshouses Bridge, which is crossed to return to Glasshouses.

Note that the presence of two sets of sewage works is not as off-putting as might be implied! (just keep your eyes right)

The former railway line is much in evidence on this walk, the forlorn viaduct's supports being a particularly sad reminder of what must have been a most attractive route. The Nidd Valley Line was opened in 1862 by the North Eastern Railway Co., mainly to assist the valley's industries. Running from near Harrogate up the valley as far as Pateley Bridge, this single-track line finally succumbed in 1964

Summerbridge is a fairly substantial village with a number of shops, including the only 'chippy' outside of Pateley (within our scope). The inn is named after a famous racehorse, and as we enter the village we are surprised by a large semi-modern thatched residence. The bridge itself is a shapely structure.

Across the river stands Dacre Banks, though all we see is the Parish Church. The Youth Hostel, one of Yorkshire's first, is the old village school.

The tributary here is Fell Beck

Knox Manor

Low Laithe

Dacre Banks

Summerbridge

sewage works

line of former railway

River Nidd

old mill weir

weir

N

WALK 4 | THE VALLEY OF HOW STEAN BECK |

3½ miles

from Middlesmoor

An assortment of ups
and downs, providing
extensive views and
fine beck scenery

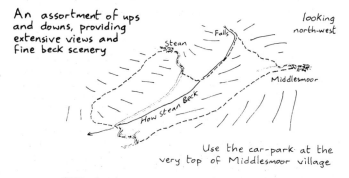

Use the car-park at the
very top of Middlesmoor village

THE WALK

From the centre of Middlesmoor make for
the church, which can be reached by any of several winding
by-ways. To the right of the churchyard will be seen a
stile, beyond which a short snicket leads to a gate. From
here a long flight of steps leads rather incongruously down
into a field, from where a normal path continues the
straight line to Halfway House farm. Go straight through
the farmyard to a gate at the far end, and then head
down the right-side of the field to a stile. Similarly a
stile is met at the bottom of the next field, before a
final field is crossed to the far left to emerge through
a stile onto the road near Lofthouse, at a lay-by.

Head along to the right but leave almost
immediately at the left fork to Stean. On crossing over
How Stean Beck, leave the road for the track left to
Studfold. Avoid the farm by remaining on the track which
swings right to climb steeply past some cottages. Ignore
a left fork and continue up the hill to the second of
two barns on the right, there taking a gate at the
top side of it.

A farm-track runs alongside the wall,
leading to Whitbeck Farm: instead of following it round
to the left-side of the buildings, take a 'slimline' gate
to the right, where just beyond it a gate empties onto
a farm-road. Now turn left up into the yard, then

20

immediately right to descend the slope to a footbridge over the beck. Through a gate at the other side, turn right along the bottom of the fields, taking in two stiles before a gate gains entry to the confines of an attractive farm building. Head straight across to a gapstile, and likewise across an open field. From there follow a wall away to a tiny footbridge which crosses a beck and leads onto the road in Stean.

Turn right down the lane as far as the first bend after leaving the hamlet, and there use a stile from where an enclosed path descends to cross over the aggressively attractive How Stean Beck. From the gate beyond, turn left on an initially sketchy path along the field bottom, improving as it crosses several stiles to enter woods alongside the beck. On reaching a stile at the far end of the wood, descend into a large meadow, with How Stean Force visible just ahead. The best viewpoint involves crossing the bridge over the inflowing tributary to draw level with the falls.

From the waterfalls retrace steps to the stile on the edge of the wood, where a second stile can be spotted only a few yards up to the left. From it climb through the bracken to a gateway, and then bear half-right to a stile in a fence. Follow a hedge away from it to another stile, then slope up across a large field to a gate. From here a track runs to the farm ahead, passing along the front of it and out onto the road at the entrance to Middlesmoor, across from the Wesleyan Chapel of 1899.

How Stean Force

How Stean Beck has made quite a name for itself due to the nature of it's activities in the Gorge, but there is much more to it than simply the confines of the tourist trap. When we meet it near Stean the rock walls already hold it tight, whilst upstream a smaller waterfall (difficult to see from the path) precedes our highlight, the Aysgarth-like **How Stean Force**

Note that the Kiln (which can easily go un-noticed from above) is in good enough repair to make an excellent shelter from the rain.

Stean

Stean is a solid farming hamlet, on it's own 'cul-de-sac'. The only public amenity is a phone box.

Middlesmoor is the last village in the dale and probably the most interesting. Built on neither the Nidd nor a tributary, but as the name suggests, it stands on the vast tongue of moorland between the How Stean valley and that of the upper Nidd. At a windswept near-1000 feet up, the residents must be a hardy breed! The solid stone cottages are interlaced by a fascinating network of alleyways, fittingly leading to the Church of St. Chad. Rebuilt in 1866, this attractive church stands on an ancient foundation, a Saxon cross in the church is said to be the 7th century preaching cross of St. Chad

Falls

How Stean Beck

Falls

Kiln →

②

③

N

Middlesmoor

the churchyard is a renowned viewpoint

Halfway House

ROAD

ROAD

lay-by

LOFTHOUSE

Whitbeck

Studfold

①

Besides the farm at Studfold, there is a school outdoor centre and a caravan-site

The old kiln

WALK 5 | THE ASCENT OF LITTLE WHERNSIDE

7¼ miles

from Scar House

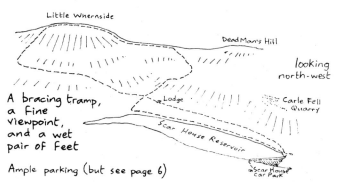

Little Whernside

Dead Man's Hill

looking
north-west

A bracing tramp,
a fine
viewpoint,
and a wet
pair of feet

Lodge

Carle Fell
Quarry

Scar House Reservoir

Scar House
Car Park

Ample parking (but see page 6)

THE WALK

From the car-park head for Scar House Reservoir and take the road across the top of the dam. At the far end, leave the track immediately and turn left along the shore of the reservoir. Initially unclear and a little damp, the path soon improves to take us along most of the length of the north shore. After the tree-girt beck flowing down from the Lodge, a 'rest-house' is reached, and from the stile just beyond, abandon the shore to climb alongside the wall.

Passing through a couple of intervening gates, a junction of walled tracks is reached: here leave them all behind and instead use a gateway on the left to take a track heading across the rough pasture. Little Whernside now looms larger and much closer. Taking in one or two rather damp sections, the path rises through two more gateways. Beyond this second one the climbing is delayed by a long almost-level march on a very indistinct path. As a result the path may easily be lost, but simply remain on roughly the same contour to reach a gate in a sturdy wall rising directly up the fellside.

Through the gate turn right to accompany the wall up a rather steep section, eventually easing to follow what is by now a fence through tall peat

Easy to locate as the only cairn on the broad Fell-top, the summit could equally be claimed by any one of a hundred other peat-castles, some of which are almost certainly higher than the chosen spot. A visit to the cairn will entail the only venture into the Yorkshire Dales National Park to be found in this book, and for that reason alone it may be judged worthwhile.

Why, oh why though couldn't the graceful rise of Little Whernside have been maintained just 200 or 300 feet more, instead of this abrupt end in a boggy plateau?

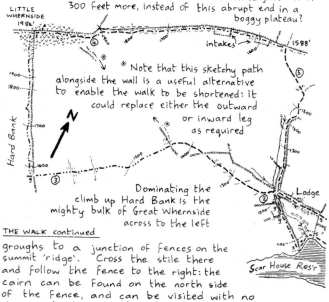

LITTLE WHERNSIDE 1984'

intakes   1588'

⑤

* Note that this sketchy path alongside the wall is a useful alternative to enable the walk to be shortened: it could replace either the outward or inward leg as required

Hard Bank

N

④

③

Dominating the climb up Hard Bank is the mighty bulk of Great Whernside across to the left

Lodge

②

Scar House Res'r

THE WALK continued

groughs to a junction of fences on the summit 'ridge'. Cross the stile there and follow the fence to the right: the cairn can be found on the north side of the fence, and can be visited with no damage to the low fence.

Back alongside the fence continue eastward through peat-castles which at times block out all other views. After a short, steep descent a longer, wetter stretch follows, until a gate in the fence signals our meeting with the Coverdale track. Turn right along it, leaving the watershed to drop down in no time at all to the junction of tracks left earlier in the day.

Here turn along the track to the left, passing the low ruins of Lodge and remaining on an excellent track to return us to the dam and from there the car-park.

Looking west from Little Whernside

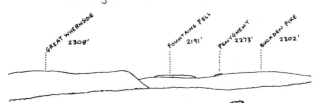

GREAT WHERNSIDE 2308'

FOUNTAINS FELL 2191'

PENYGHENT 2273'

BUCKDEN PIKE 2302'

Visible from the summit are the four major tops of the south-eastern Dales. Further highlights of Little Whernside's views include the rolling hills above Wensleydale and points north, while closer to hand the shapely Penhill rises above the verdant green floor of Coverdale. Note the splendid patchwork of fields behind the farmstead of Woodale, at the head of Coverdale almost at our feet.

Now a complete ruin, the Lodge is thought to be on the site of a medieval hunting lodge. It now provides just about the only foliage to be seen on this walk. Of the ways that leave here, of most interest is the old packhorse road from Coverdale (which we use to return to here). From it's summit can be seen ahead a shooting-box on Dead Man's Hill, so named because of the discovery, 250 years ago, of the bodies of three Scottish pedlars buried in the peat.

← High above us here is Carle Fell Quarry

Scar House Reservoir

From the dam our target of Little Whernside is clearly in view, to the right and in front of the mass of Great Whernside

Our walk along the reservoir shore follows the course of a long-dismantled tramway. Used in reservoir construction, it ran to the foot of Angram dam.

River Nidd

Car Park

LOFTHOUSE

N

WALK 6

| SCOT GATE ASH QUARRY AND WATH |

4 miles

From Pateley Bridge

looking north-east

Wath

Quarries

An easy-to-follow
route on what is
virtually a rural
history trail

River Nidd

Pateley
Bridge

Use the main car-park
in Pateley Bridge

THE WALK

From the car-park head up the
High Street, turning left along Church Street. Past
the church continue straight ahead on Wath Road.
After the last house on the left, the road crosses
a bridge: this is the course of the old inclined
tramway serving the quarry. By using the stile
on the right we can follow it's steep, unswerving
course all the way up to the old workings on
the hilltop.

With the remains of the terminal
of the tramway directly ahead, a track heads
away to the left, keeping close company with
the fence/wall there. This clear path skirts the lower
boundary of the quarry's heathery environs to
eventually reach a gate. From the stile there,
cross the field to a similar combination which
deposits us onto a narrow lane.

This quiet by-way is followed downhill
with magnificent views up the valley to Gouthwaite
Reservoir. Continue straight ahead at a junction
and this lane will lead unerringly into Wath.
Follow it round to the left, past the hotel to
the narrow bridge over the Nidd. Our return
leg commences at the footbridge on the left,
immediately before the bridge. From it a path
heads straight across the meadow to a stile,
continuing similarly across the next field to join

the unmistakeable course of the former railway.

After another stile adjacent to the line, the line is then followed for some distance to the point where the river comes within a handful of yards. Beyond a stile in this tree-shrouded setting we now forsake the line for the river, it's attractive tree-lined bank being our route back into Pateley Bridge. On reaching a weir the path becomes confined by fences and is deflected away from the river to emerge between buildings onto a short lane immediately adjacent to Pateley's graceful bridge.

Wath — a delightful name!

In the surprisingly extensive Scot Gate Ash Quarries was won 'delphstone', a particularly strong stone which went towards the construction of some of London's major buildings. Imagine the spectacle of the stone being lowered 600 feet down the ingenius tramway to the railway yard

RAMSGILL

PATELEY BRIDGE

② Pie Gill Green

PATELEY BRIDGE

N ↑

River Nidd

line of former railway ③

PATELEY BRIDGE

Pateley Moor

Scot Gate Ash Quarry ①

The descent to Pie Gill Green on the lane from the quarry provides marvellous views up the valley to Gouthwaite Reservoir and beyond.

viewpoint for Ashfold Side Beck, Greenhow Hill and the unsightly objects on Menwith Hill

site of former tramway (note the gradient)

Note the lively confluence here with Foster Beck, with a green island in the centre

weir

Pateley Bridge

RIPON B6265
SUMMERBRIDGE B6165

GRASSINGTON B6265 ← Wath Bridge

27

WALK 7 | ABOVE THE NIDD TO LOFTHOUSE

5½ miles

from Ramsgill

A superb circuit above the river, commanding extensive views in all directions

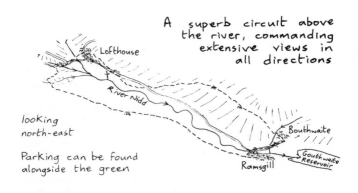

looking
north-east

Parking can be found
alongside the green

THE WALK

Boots are likely to be rendered muddy within five minutes of the start: take the up-dale (Lofthouse) road to the smaller-scale green, at the opposite side of which our path to Lofthouse sets off through a farmyard. From the gate at the far end a good path heads away through the fields. After five stiles or gates our accompanying field boundary changes over to the left, and after passing a large barn the path climbs to West House farm.

Skirting round the right of it's confines our path heads directly away, ignoring the farm access-track which drops away to the right. Now becoming a little sketchier the path encounters three more stiles/gates on the level before swinging a little right to a stile. A grassy rake then heads away to join another farm-track: this takes us down to a bridge over Blayshaw Gill and on to a T-junction of walled tracks. Turning right our track descends and swings left to join the cul-de-sac road to Stean.

Turn right over a bridge and past the Middlesmoor junction to a lay-by: here take a wicket-gate, passing to the right of a barn and left of a cricket pitch to a similar gate. Cross straight over the water-board road to use a footbridge over the Nidd, from where a path to the right deposits us into the attractive centre of Lofthouse.

To commence the return leg, turn right for a short distance before entering the hotel car-park, there using an unlikely-looking gate on the right to enter a field alongside the hotel grounds. Head half-left to use a stile cleverly incorporated into a wall: follow it right to a stile, from there heading across a field to another stile and down onto the road at Nidd Heads. After five minutes on the road take a stile on the right, heading half-right to a stile well beyond a barn. From the next stile by a rusting barn the old railway line is encountered: a wicket-gate just ahead gains access to the track-way, which takes us back onto the road just short of a bridge over the river.

Just across the road a stile quickly returns us to the fields. Follow the pronounced way of the railway to a gate, then climb half-left on a sketchy track to another gate. Past a third gate at the same angle the slope eases, and heading away from it an enclosed path is joined at a small gate to take us to Longside House. Our path passes between the trees and the rear of the house, going on through a gate to Longside Farm.

Again keeping round the back, a sketchy path contours across to a choice of ladder-stile or foot-gate, then accompanies the right-hand field boundary to another stile. From it drop steeply to a gap-stile, a farm bridge taking us into the hamlet of Bouthwaite. Go ahead to a junction of lanes, there turning right to the junction at Nidd Bridge on the edge of Ramsgill.

Nidd Heads

29

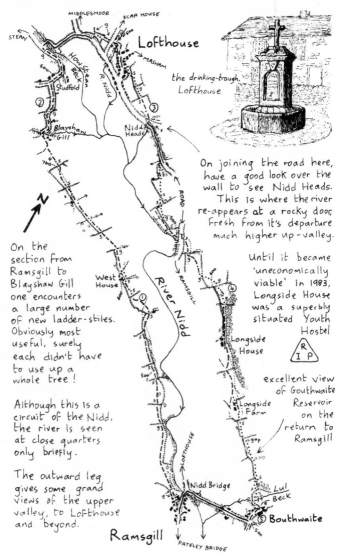

⑦

MIDDLESMOOR SCAR HOUSE

STEAN

Lofthouse

How Stean Beck

R. Nidd

MASHAM

Studfold

②

Blayshaw Gill

Nidd Heads

②

the drinking-trough, Lofthouse

N

West House

River Nidd

ROAD

RAMSGILL

Longside House

Longside Farm

LOFTHOUSE

gap

Nidd Bridge

Lul Beck

⑥ Bouthwaite

Ramsgill

PATELEY BRIDGE

On joining the road here,
have a good look over the
wall to see Nidd Heads.
This is where the river
re-appears at a rocky door,
fresh from it's departure
much higher up-valley.

Until it became
'uneconomically
viable' in 1983,
Longside House
was a superbly
situated Youth
Hostel
R I P

excellent view
of Gouthwaite
Reservoir
on the
return to
Ramsgill

On the
section from
Ramsgill to
Blayshaw Gill
one encounters
a large number
of new ladder-stiles.
Obviously most
useful, surely
each didn't have
to use up a
whole tree !

Although this is a
circuit of the Nidd,
the river is seen
at close quarters
only briefly.

The outward leg
gives some grand
views of the upper
valley, to Lofthouse
and beyond.

WALK 8

8¼ miles

FOUNTAINS EARTH MOOR

from Ramsgill

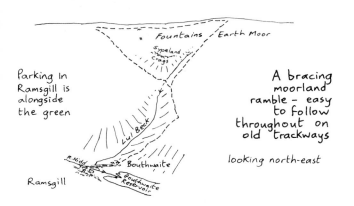

Parking in Ramsgill is alongside the green

A bracing moorland ramble – easy to follow throughout on old trackways

looking north-east

THE WALK

From the village green take the road north towards Lofthouse, but immediately after crossing Nidd Bridge take the narrow lane to Bouthwaite. At the junction of tracks at the end, go straight ahead to a gate beyond which a stony track climbs the hillside. When the gradient eventually eases the track becomes much more pleasant underfoot, rising through several gates until a junction is reached at a wall-corner. Take the left branch for a level trek to arrive at another fork, with a choice of two gates. This is the point to which we shall later return.

Opt for the right fork: the track rises very gradually through the heather, passing through another gate before arriving at a T-junction. Here turn left for a level march past a substantial shooting-house, through a gate and on to another T-junction. Here we turn left once more, on a superb green road for the most part enclosed by walls. In due course it leads us down to rejoin our outward track at the two gates.

The return to Ramsgill is by simply retracing our earlier steps, a most pleasureable task.

The green,
Ramsgill,
showing the
Yorke Arms from
the horse trough

➡ Z

Ramsgill

→ LOFTHOUSE

PATELEY BRIDGE

R. Nidd
Nidd Bridge

Bouthwaite

During the
climb from
Bouthwaite
the view
beyond Ramsgill
to the valley
of Ramsgill
Beck is most
appealing ~ this is
another of Nidderdale's
forbidden places.

Bouthwaite is Ramsgill's smaller
neighbour across the river, but is
by no means as far as the signpost
at Nidd Bridge suggests. Here the
monks of Fountains Abbey
had their grange. Close
neighbours in so much of
Nidderdale, they were also apparently
good neighbours with the brothers
from Byland who needed to pass
through here to return to
their more distant abbey.
On the lane into
Bouthwaite we see a
small Wesleyan Chapel
dated 1890.

remains of
guide-post (relatively modern)

Ramsgill is a
beautifully-sited village
on the banks of it's own
beck, just short of the
confluence with the Nidd. The
prime feature is the spacious green
through which the valley-road runs. Some fine cottages
play supporting role to the striking ivy-clad hotel that rule
the green. Since extended, the hotel was once a shooting
lodge of the Yorke family, and still bears their name. In
earlier times Ramsgill was a grange of Byland Abbey, an
at the rear of the church is a solitary gable-end, all tha
now remains. The solid-looking church was rebuilt in 1843, and
looks out across the reedy head of Gouthwaite Reservoir.

Our stride across the moor-top — which it goes without saying should be reserved for late summer — is likely to reveal a great deal more moorland than may have been expected. Stretching away to the east is a vast tract of superb upland, criss-crossed by trackways but free from motor-roads. Some of these are of ancient origin, indeed our climb out of Bouthwaite is along the very way used by the monks on the march to and from their abbeys. Since then this road was still important as the start of the way to Masham and Kirkby Malzeard. Strangely enough, both tracks leading east from the now-defunct guide-post (see map opposite) were both designated as good, metalled roads for traffic as recently as the late 1950's. Happily of course they are actually traffic-free, save for the occasional grouse-shooters.

Jenny Twigg and her Daughter Tib

Sad to say, the two best individual features of the walk are on private land, but for the very keen, these remarkable stones can be seen and reached from the gate by the shooting-house, while the impressive range of Sypeland Crags — which can already be seen to good advantage — can be seen at close hand by one or two obvious ways

→ Z

Sypeland Gill

Jenny Twigg and her Daughter Tib

stone shooting house

Fountains Earth Moor

Sypeland Crags

Lul Beck

guide stone

Inscribed boundary stone

Sypeland Crags

33

WALK 9

6½ miles

BRIMHAM ROCKS AND FELL BECK

from Low Laithe

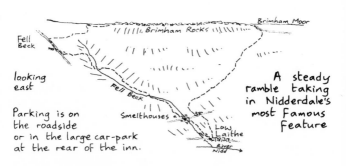

Fell Beck

looking east

Parking is on the roadside or in the large car-park at the rear of the inn.

Brimham Moor

Brimham Rocks

Fell Beck

Smelthouses

Low Laithe

River Nidd

A steady ramble taking in Nidderdale's most famous feature

THE WALK

Almost opposite the inn a bridle-way heads away from the road. Follow it up until it joins a lane, turning left only as far as the last house, there using the drive on the right. Just past the attractive range of buildings at Low Wood House, the track swings left: here leave it by a gate on the right to follow a wide green track rising very gradually. For a while completely enclosed, the track later follows a fence to arrive at a gate where High Wood comes up to meet us. Beyond the gate a path heads up through the pasture to a gateway in the wall on the right, then soon leaves the trees to rise to the left. Through another gateway and alongside a field (typical 'Brimham country' now dominant on our left), one more gate is met before emerging onto the road.

Head left along the road as it crosses Brimham Moor, and leave it along the drive to the visitor's car-park. Followed past the car-park it will lead directly to Brimham House, but to experience the Rocks more intimately, turn off at the information board by the car-park on the left along a well-made footpath. This passes right through the heart of things and has many off-shoots to explore the features, eventually coming out across from Brimham House.

Leave by a footpath round to the left, which branches off the drive just short of the House.

34

Yet more splendid outcrops are encountered, and past the last one the path loops back to the right. Here leave it by a narrow green path which maintains our northerly aim and drops down to join a wider path. Turn left along this, and, bearing left at the next fork it will lead onto a farm access-road on the edge of the moor.

Head left along this farm-road through woods, leaving it at a gate on the right shortly after the trees end. With no visible path head straight along the field, through a gateway and on to a gate in the far corner on the right, in front of North Pasture Farm. Another gate admits to the yard, which is vacated by a gate on the left, after the main buildings but before the modern barn

Aim to the right across the field, pathless again but with a line of telegraph poles as an infallible guide. Beyond a fence our line continues to reach a good track at a gate. Once through it, take the first gate on the right to follow an enclosed track down over a beck and up onto the Pateley Bridge - Ripon road. A left turn leads down to the inn at Fell Beck.

From the inn remain on the road as far as the first farm-road off to the left: pass between the buildings to a gate then swing right to another. Descend by the wall to a stile, then turn right above the beck to a gate. Now a clearer path through the trees remains above the beck as far as the next fence from the stile there it drops down to accompany the beck as far as a walled track from the right. Here use the gate on the left to go down to a footbridge, then turning right on a path which rises gradually through the trees.

Passing in and out of a field the path soon reaches the rear of the buildings at Low Wood. Climb to the left to leave the trees by a gate, then almost at once turn right to drop down along the front of the farm buildings. Beyond a stile the path swings left: ignore the branch down to the beck, but remain level to enter deep into the woods. Our path eventually meets another, just past a stile. Follow it down to the right to cross a footbridge over the beck, then simply follow it downstream to emerge via a gate onto the lane through Smelthouses.

Turn left over the bridge, then take the wide track on the right which accompanies the beck down onto the road in Low Laithe. A left turn returns us to the village centre.

Barely even a hamlet, Fell Beck stands where
the beck from which it is named is bridged
by the Ripon-Pateley Bridge road. Standing
next to the beck is
the Half Moon Inn,
which hosts the local
harvest festival in
late September.

Fell Beck is a lively
watercourse flowing
through magnificent
wooded surroundings.
It has been put
to good use by
local industry in
times past, providing
several features of
interest. Below the
higher dam is seen
a 10-tier weir, with
another weir and
pond passed
lower down.

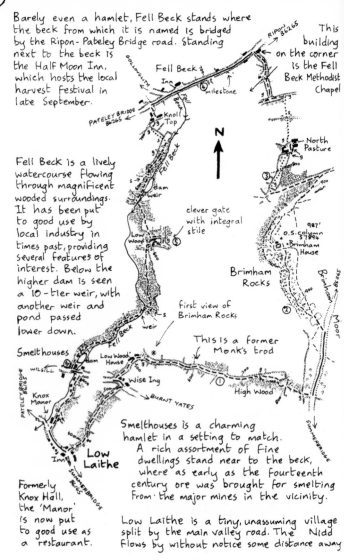

This
building
on the corner
is the Fell
Beck Methodist
Chapel

Smelthouses is a charming
hamlet in a setting to match.
A rich assortment of fine
dwellings stand near to the beck,
where as early as the fourteenth
century ore was brought for smelting
from the major mines in the vicinity.

Formerly
Knox Hall,
the 'Manor'
is now put
to good use as
a restaurant.

Low Laithe is a tiny, unassuming village
split by the main valley road. The Nidd
flows by without notice some distance away

36

9

Brimham Rocks are the pride of Nidderdale, a magnet for visitors and a must on the best itineraries: indeed, if tourists see nothing else of the valley they'll come here, before moving on to Fountains Abbey, Ripon and the like. This is a popular destination for school trips, and is indeed an absolute paradise for energetic youngsters.

The magnificent Rocks are immense blocks of millstone-grit, sculptured by the natural savagery of the elements. Perched at 900 feet above sea-level, these strongly individual boulders look down upon the wide valley bottom, from where they form a fine serrated skyline. This jumble of rocks are spread across an area of 50 to 60 acres on the edge of Brimham Moor. Once owned by the monks of Fountains Abbey, the estate spent more than 160 years in the possession of Grantley Hall, before it was left to the National Trust by a private individual in 1970, as part of the near-400 acre Brimham Moor.

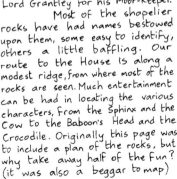

The Idol

In their usual skilled way the Trust have tidied up the environs of the rocks, improving car-parking, visitor facilities and paths. Toilets and refreshments are provided alongside the shop/information centre in Brimham House. The 'Rocks House' was built in 1792 by Lord Grantley for his moor-keeper.

Most of the shapelier rocks have had names bestowed upon them, some easy to identify, others a little baffling. Our route to the House is along a modest ridge, from where most of the rocks are seen. Much entertainment can be had in locating the various characters, from the Sphinx and the Cow to the Baboon's Head and the Crocodile. Originally this page was to include a plan of the rocks, but why take away half of the fun? (it was also a beggar to map)

The Dancing Bear

37

WALK 10 | ANGRAM AND SCAR HOUSE RESERVOIRS

4½ miles

from Scar House

A very easy level circuit of
Scar House Reservoir at
the bleak valley head

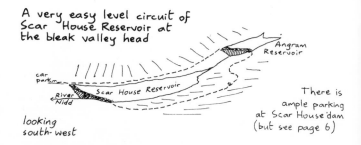

car park

River Nidd

Scar House Reservoir

Angram Reservoir

There is
ample parking
at Scar House dam
(but see page 6)

looking
south-west

THE WALK

From the car-park join the water-
board road which runs past the dam of Scar House
Reservoir (do not cross it) and along the full length
of it's southern shore, to eventually reach the foot
of Angram Reservoir. Cross the dam and take a
sketchy path heading immediately off to the right
from an old kissing-gate.

After a slight descent, the path
makes it's way on the level past long-collapsed walls
to a gate, another gateway and, just before a fence,
a gap in the wall alongside. From the corner beyond,
an enclosed track rises then swings sharp right to the
unmistakeable cluster of trees around the ruins of Lodge.
This same track now leads high above Scar House shore
back to the dam which is this time crossed to return
us to the
car-park.

Angram Dam
and Great
Whernside

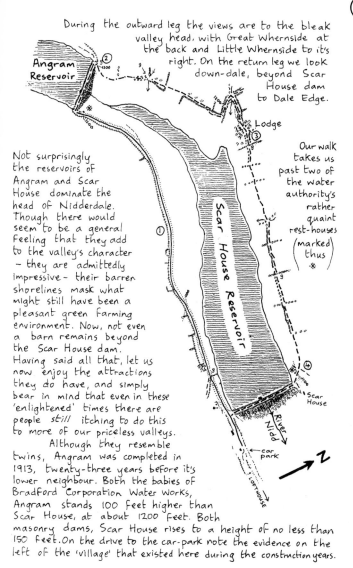

During the outward leg the views are to the bleak valley head, with Great Whernside at the back and Little Whernside to it's right. On the return leg we look down-dale, beyond Scar House dam to Dale Edge.

Angram Reservoir

②
1200

Lodge
③

Scar House Reservoir

Our walk takes us past two of the water authority's rather quaint rest-houses (marked thus) *

①

④

Scar House

River Nidd

car park

N →

LOFT HOUSE

Not surprisingly the reservoirs of Angram and Scar House dominate the head of Nidderdale. Though there would seem to be a general feeling that they add to the valley's character – they are admittedly impressive – their barren shorelines mask what might still have been a pleasant green farming environment. Now, not even a barn remains beyond the Scar House dam. Having said all that, let us now enjoy the attractions they do have, and simply bear in mind that even in these 'enlightened' times there are people *still* itching to do this to more of our priceless valleys.

Although they resemble twins, Angram was completed in 1913, twenty-three years before it's lower neighbour. Both the babies of Bradford Corporation Water Works, Angram stands 100 feet higher than Scar House, at about 1200 feet. Both masonry dams, Scar House rises to a height of no less than 150 feet. On the drive to the car-park note the evidence on the left of the 'village' that existed here during the construction years.

WALK 11

6¾ miles

ASHFOLD SIDE and MERRYFIELD MINES

from Pateley Bridge

Well-defined tracks lead
both to and from a
fascinating objective.
Extensive views of
the Pateley area

Use the main
car-park in
Pateley Bridge

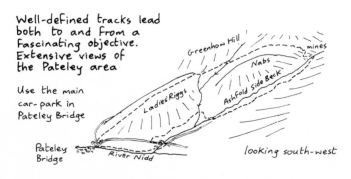

looking south-west

THE WALK

From the car-park cross the bridge and
turn immediately into the park on the right. Staying
along the wooded riverbank, a good path leads through
the first caravan site of the day before reaching open
fields. In the second field the path cuts the corner at
Foster Beck's entry into the Nidd, to a stile to the right
of the prominent Brigg House farm. Alongside a cottage
a small footbridge transports us over the beck, which is
followed upstream to a gate before striking across to
another gate at a junction of lanes.

Turn left along the lane, past the inn
with it's water-wheel to a sharp bend: here a farm-track
leaves the road and it should be followed all the
way to Mosscarr Farm, ignoring an uphill left fork
on the way. Continuing behind the farm (which stands
strangely island-like in the middle of a field) the track
continues to a cottage, just beyond which is a
footbridge. Head downstream a few yards before striking
away between enclosing walls to a track above Ashfold
Side Beck. Turn right to descend to a bridge to take
us onto a farm-road next to a caravan site.

This strip of tarmac is followed up to
the left, clusters of caravans now appearing with
regularity. At a steep fork to Westfield House farm,
remain on the level track to enter a caravan site. Our

track threads it's way through to finally shrug off the last caravan just when it seemed we'd never be free of them. This same track takes us all the way up the valley to eventually reach the site of the old mines which suddenly appear across the beck in dramatic fashion. A footpath breaks off from the track to drop down to a gate, beyond which a concrete ford with it's own stepping-stones takes us across the beck.

Behind the large ruinous building is the prominent steep line of the old flue — at it's foot a narrow green path heads half-left through the heather to join a wide track. Turning right along it, the flue is again met below the remains of an old chimney. From here the track heads through the centre of the mines, at the foot of the main spoil-heaps. At the wall at the far side we turn left, and the track at first a little sketchily starts to climb above the site, levelling out before reaching a gate.

Beyond it the track continues alongside a wall to arrive at Brandstone Dub Bridge, crossing it and heading away again in confident manner. Several farms are passed by as our way 'improves' into a narrow tarmac lane. About five minutes beyond Riggs House farm on lofty Ladies' Rigg, the lane enters a shroud of trees: here leave it through the few trees on the left to a stile in a corner. From it follow the hedge downhill with Pateley Bridge directly ahead.

Keeping the field boundary on the right, two gates are encountered before joining a back-road at Bridgehouse Gate, from where the river is re-crossed to return to the car-park in Pateley Bridge.

The Watermill, Foster Beck

The splendid waterwheel alongside Foster Beck is visible to all from the road. No less than 35 feet in diameter, this iron and wood structure formerly operated a hemp mill which was still in production until relatively recently. The mill itself has now been converted into an inn, but sadly the wheel shows little sign of being preserved at the moment.

The short-lived Foster Beck is a result of Ashfold Side Beck and Brandstone Beck meeting.

note the attractive waterfall just below shapely Brandstone Dub Bridge

From here is an excellent view of Pateley's High Street rising, it would seem, vertically

this lane gives a drier and slightly quicker finish

Merryfield Mines provide a marvellous insight into the dale's important lead-mining past. Even the track we take to it is a typically well-engineered mine-road. Below is a brief plan to show several features of interest. Take care when exploring!

highest point of Ladies' Riggs (fine view across the valley to Brimham Rocks)

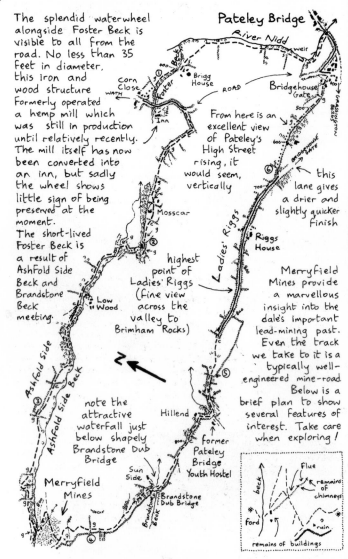

Pateley Bridge

River Nidd

weir

Corn Close

WATH

Brigg House

ROAD

Bridgehouse Gate

Inn

Mosscar

Ladies' Riggs

Riggs House

Low Wood

Ashfold Side

Ashfold Side Beck

Merryfield Mines

Sun Side

Hillend

former Pateley Bridge Youth Hostel

Brandstone Dub Bridge

Brandstone Beck

beck
Flue
remains of chimneys
ford
ruin
remains of buildings

WALK 12
9 miles

SCAR HOUSE AND DALE EDGE

from Middlesmoor

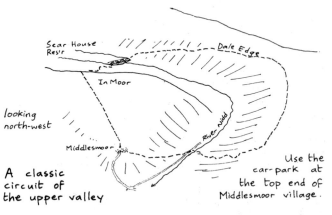

Scar House Res'r

Dale Edge

In Moor

looking north-west

Middlesmoor

River Nidd

A classic circuit of the upper valley

Use the car-park at the top end of Middlesmoor village.

THE WALK

Leave the car-park by turning right along the lane, which immediately degenerates into a track. This wide stony way leads us unceasingly but gradually upwards, eventually levelling out on the moor-top. Beyond a gate our track now runs free, before descending to the water-board road on the south shore of Scar House Reservoir. Turn right as far as the dam then cross it, taking the track immediately ahead. Just past the 'rest-house' branch right on a good path which rises to a gate. A little beyond, marshy ground is encountered, but the path soon picks up to continue to another gate before dropping down to cross Woo Gill and a tributary in quick succession.

Shortly after vacating their deep confines, forsake the wide track for a lesser path climbing to a prominent little spoil heap on the left. Here, at an old shaft, a good path again heads away to the right, and this is the commencement of an almost level trek round Dale Edge. With magnificent views and a superb path the whole way, no instructions are necessary as we contour round the large loop of the valley to eventually arrive at the unmistakeable shooting-house above Thrope Edge.

Just before the shooting-house a path zig-zags down to a gate, then heads a little more gently to the left before swinging sharp right on reaching a wood. Take the gate at the bottom and follow the fence away left to a gate in it, there descending to a barn and onto the track behind Thrope Farm. Turn right and then sharp left into the farmyard, going to the right of the farm to take a track down to the river: cross the bridge and rise to the water-board road.

Follow this to the left as far as a stile on the right, then head diagonally across several fields with prominent stiles ahead. From a narrow wood aim across a large field, locating two more stiles and then a gate to re-enter Middlesmoor near the Church.

This reclaimed field looks curiously out of place on the open fell

From this deep shaft down which water can be heard dripping, one has the rare opportunity to survey all three of Nidderdale's reservoirs.

Fold

shaft

⑤

shaft

Woo Gill

④

Mine Shaft above Woo Gill

The steep descent to Scar House permits sweeping views of the area: on the opposite side of the valley are the extensive Carle Fell quarries

Rain Stang

N

Scar House
③
River Nidd
rest house
LOFTHOUSE

Scar House Reservoir

②
WOO GILL

cairn

44

old quarry

Dale Edge

remains of a cross
or guide-post?

At this
crossroads of
tracks is an
inscribed stone,
now weathered
illegible: the
other track
leads over
the moor
towards
Masham

Surely there are
easier ways of discarding
of old cookers than carting
them up to a quarry at 1475 feet?

On the long stride around Dale Edge
the views along the length of the dale
rank superlatives: a fine contrast is
formed by the green of the valley at
our feet and the dark outlines of the
rounded Meugher and the two Whernsides.

The shooting-house
above Thrope Edge,
which from the
water-board road
far below appears
to be a church

N

⑦

Thrope Edge

shooting
house

SCAR HOUSE

Thrope
Farm

River Nidd

LOFTHOUSE

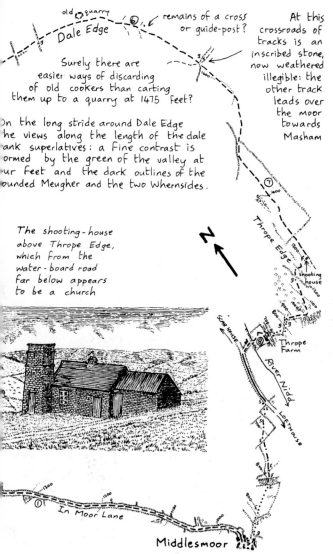

① In Moor Lane

1300

Middlesmoor

WALK 13

FISHPOND WOOD AND LOW MOOR

3½ miles

from Bewerley

A gentle exploration
of the highly-varied
hinterland of
Bewerley

There is adequate
roadside parking
near the green

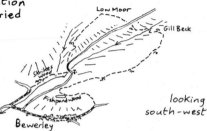

looking
south-west

THE WALK

From the telephone-box in Bewerley
head back along the road to Pateley Bridge, forking
left at the first junction on a lane climbing out
of the village. After a couple of minutes, take a
stile on the left opposite a barn. Head directly up
the field, through a collapsed wall to the very top,
there being deflected right to a gap-stile. A left
turn here descends to enter Fishpond Wood via a
kissing-gate. A path heads into the heart of the
wood alongside a tiny stream which is crossed by
a plank-bridge before we reach the 'lakeshore'.

On leaving it's bank our path meets
a wider track: turn right along it to swing round
to a wicket-gate alongside a lane. Here we leave
the wood, but without setting foot on the tarmac
head up the winding farm-track to the right. This
ever-rising track can now be followed unerringly
past three farms (only entering the actual confines
of the third) and along to a fourth one. On
approaching the fourth farm, Gillbeck, turn left
through a gate just before the first barn, on a
track which descends to ford a beck.

Almost immediately after this ford
leave the track to climb the pathless grass slope
to the right, locating a stile just on the left of
the cottage at the top. From the private-looking

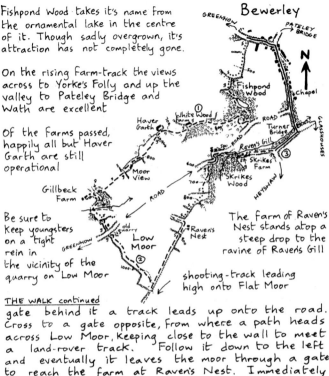

Bewerley

Fishpond Wood takes it's name from the ornamental lake in the centre of it. Though sadly overgrown, it's attraction has not completely gone.

On the rising farm-track the views across to Yorke's Folly and up the valley to Pateley Bridge and Wath are excellent

Of the farms passed, happily all but Haver Garth are still operational

Be sure to keep youngsters on a tight rein in the vicinity of the quarry on Low Moor

The farm of Raven's Nest stands atop a steep drop to the ravine of Raven's Gill

shooting-track leading high onto Flat Moor

THE WALK continued

gate behind it a track leads up onto the road. Cross to a gate opposite, from where a path heads across Low Moor, keeping close to the wall to meet a land-rover track. Follow it down to the left and eventually it leaves the moor through a gate to reach the farm at Raven's Nest. Immediately after turning sharp left in front of the house, take a stile on the right to descend by a wall through two further stiles. From the latter, a path takes us steeply down through bracken to a gate onto a lane.

Beyond an S-bend a gate on the right admits to Skrikes Wood. After a footbridge over a beck, a path runs along the bottom of the wood to leave it by a stile: just ahead is Skrikes Farm. Use a gate in the wall on the left to pass round to the left of the main buildings. A track is joined by a gate to head away on the farm-drive out onto a lane. Turn left to a junction at Turner Bridge and left again back up into Bewerley.

WALK 14

3½ miles

from Lofthouse

An easy
to follow
ramble,
making a
circuit of
a visit to the
magnificent
Gorge

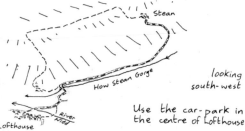

looking
south-west

Use the car-park in
the centre of Lofthouse

THE WALK

Leave Lofthouse by a track between the
cottages by the water-trough, this being just across the road
from the Post Office. Got all that? Right then, a path
descends to cross a footbridge over the Nidd, after which
we cross straight over the water-board road to a wicket-
gate. Passing between the cricket pitch and a barn, a
similar gate will be seen in the wall-corner ahead. Here
the road is joined at a lay-by. Turn right for a few yards
only, and then left on the fork to Stean.

Immediately after bridging How Stean Beck
forsake the road for the farm-track left to Studfold:
avoid the farm by remaining on the track which swings
right to climb steeply past cottages. Ignore a left fork
and continue to rise, passing two more barns. Enclosed
by walls this wide track bends right to lead us without
difficulty past a branch to Moor House Farm, and
later another branch left. Just beyond is a branch to
the right: this we take to descend into the hamlet
of Stean.

Our track improves into a lane by which
we leave Stean to descend again towards How Stean Gorge.
Passing How Stean Tunnel on the right, the entrance to the
Gorge is soon reached. An entrance fee is payable at the
cafe there, and after an exploration (details opposite)
we are deposited back onto the road. Continue down to the
bridge, and from there back to Lofthouse along the lane.

How Stean Gorge is a marvellous natural spectacle, and justifiably famous. The Gorge is a limestone ravine up to eighty feet deep in places and half a mile long. The rocks have been worn into dramatic contours by the action of the water over the centuries, and deep, dark and wet caves abound. An entry fee is payable at either the cafe or the cottage, and this entitles one to explore. at will the confines of the best part of the Gorge.

The entire walk is only a short expedition, but the section downstream of the cafe is particularly exciting, where the path crosses dramatically-hung bridges to guarded natural walkways through the rocks. Of perhaps most interest are How Stean Tunnel, near the upper limit of the walk, and Tom Taylor's Chamber, where Roman coins were found last century. This 530' cave runs from the Gorge to the field behind the cafe, and can be easily negotiated with the aid of a torch, even by novices, like us.

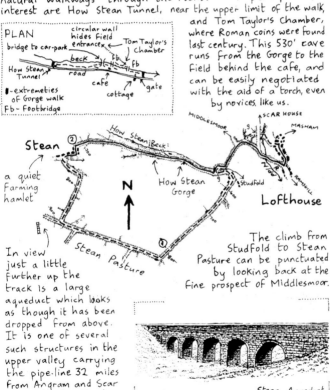

PLAN
bridge to car-park
circular wall hides field
entrance — Tom Taylor's Chamber
beck
How Stean Tunnel
road
cafe
cottage
gate
fb   fb
■ - extremeties of Gorge walk
Fb - Footbridge

Stean
a quiet Farming hamlet
How Stean Beck
How Stean Gorge
N
Stean Pasture
MIDDLESMOOR
SCAR HOUSE
MASHAM
Studfold
Lofthouse

The climb from Studfold to Stean Pasture can be punctuated by looking back at the fine prospect of Middlesmoor.

In view just a little further up the track is a large aqueduct which looks as though it has been dropped from above. It is one of several such structures in the upper valley carrying the pipe-line 32 miles from Angram and Scar House to Bradford.

Stean Aqueduct

49

WALK 15

3 miles

PANORAMA WALK AND GLASSHOUSES

from Pateley Bridge

looking east

Pateley Bridge

River Nidd

Glasshouses

pond

A very straightforward
walk which lives up to it's name
and is suitable for all weathers

Use the main car-park in Pateley Bridge

THE WALK

From the main car-park walk up the
High Street and round the sharp bend to the right,
from where it levels out. After about 150 yards, look
for a flight of steps on the left between housing
marked by a blue urban-style signpost testifying to
the popularity of the 'Panorama Walk'. A tarmac path
enclosed by walls heads steeply upwards, passing the
entrance to the cemetary; immediately after can be
found the walled way leading to the ruined church of
St. Mary. A detour thereto is a must.

Back on the main track the gradient
soon eases and with the way remaining surfaced the
fine views can be fully appreciated whilst you walk -
look out on the right for an old iron gate, behind
which is a good old-fashioned 'viewing-station'. On
reaching the tidy farming hamlet of Knott, our track
widens into a lane which soon drops down onto the
main road. After two minutes walking along to the left
(footpath provided) take a wicket-gate on the opposite
side, just past a solitary dwelling. A flagged path
leads us down to a second field, at the bottom
of which we enter Glasshouses.

Turning left along a rough road, look
for a well-enclosed snicket on the right to by-pass
a small corner of the village. On rejoining the road,
continue down past the former railway station to

arrive at a rather basic metal bridge over the Nidd. Having surveyed the river and the substantial mill-front overlooking it, retrace steps a few yards to the gateway of a private drive: this is our return route.

Even the most hapless navigator cannot go astray here. At first sandwiched between a large pond and a mill-race, the track soon meets the river at a weir. From here we follow the Nidd upstream on a path that is largely concreted, such is its usage, to arrive back in Pateley Bridge at the very bridge itself.

The 'Panorama Walk' is a popular short expedition from Pateley Bridge. Although most walks in this book include equally good views, none are as easily accessible to all. The best feature is the prospect of Guise Cliff straight across the valley. Gouthwaite Reservoir can also be seen.

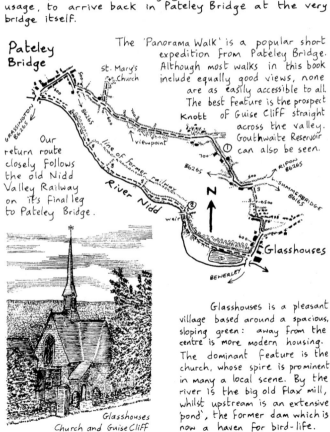

Pateley Bridge

Our return route closely follows the old Nidd Valley Railway on it's final leg to Pateley Bridge.

Glasshouses Church and Guise Cliff

Glasshouses is a pleasant village based around a spacious, sloping green: away from the centre is more modern housing. The dominant feature is the church, whose spire is prominent in many a local scene. By the river is the big old flax mill, whilst upstream is an extensive 'pond', the former dam which is now a haven for bird-life.

Pateley Bridge is the undisputed 'capital' of Nidderdale; a thriving little town that is the hub of the dale's life. Here are several inns, shops galore and generally all the facilities to satisfy most visitors. The feature which attracts immediate attention is the High Street,

The Bridge, Pateley

a narrow road which climbs at a right-angle away from the River Nidd. Virtually all the shops are spread along this thriving thoroughfare which also carries the through traffic on the Skipton to Ripon route

Across the old bridge with it's majestic twin-arches is the 'hamlet' of Bridgehouse Gate, strictly in Bewerley's extensive parish but really a part of Pateley. From here the up-dale road begins it's long, winding journey: this is truly the gateway to Upper Nidderdale. Here also are the major garage services of the valley, a useful cafe and a fine example of a local brewery. The main part is still intact but unfortunately it no longer fulfils it's original purpose.

Pateley was granted a market charter in the fourteenth century, but now only a fortnightly livestock sale takes place. However, a major one-day event is Pateley Show, held on the last Monday of September. As always, farming plays an important role hereabouts, but some of the larger sources of employment have disappeared. Pateley was once the centre of the local lead-mining industry, while quarrying and railways at one time helped support each other. Very difficult to believe today maybe, but at one time Pateley boasted two railway stations: firstly there was the terminus of the branch from Harrogate, while the Bradford Corporation line started here on it's journey to the reservoir construction at the dale-head.

The parish church is a prominent structure near the top of the town, and it typifies this millstone-grit area. Dedicated to St. Cuthbert in the 19th century, it replaced the church of St. Mary, which was much higher still. Dating from the 13th century, it is now a roof-less ruin in a superb setting. Further interest is found in the Nidderdale Museum, housed in the council offices.

WALK 16

7½ miles

GREAT HAW AND SOUTH HAW

from Scar House

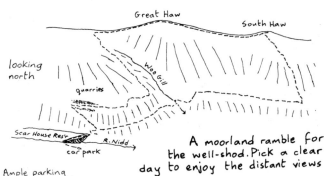

looking
north

Great Haw

South Haw

Woo Gill

quarries

Scar House Res'r

car park

R. Nidd

A moorland ramble for
the well-shod. Pick a clear
day to enjoy the distant views

Ample parking
(but see page 6)

THE WALK

From the water authority car-park
take the track to the dam of Scar House Reservoir
and head across it. At the far end take the wide
stony track up to the left, leaving it along the
bridle-path to the right opposite a 'rest-house', this
track in turn being forsaken for a very steep one
to the left signposted 'Private Road'. With increasingly
good views of the two reservoirs, the track eases
out on reaching the lower level of Carlefell Quarry,
doubling back on itself at the far end to pass
through the heart of the old workings.

On leaving the devastation the track
forks: keep to the right to pass a much smaller quarry
after which the track begins to rise across the
moor to reach a junction. Opt for the gently-
rising track to the left, with the rounded top of
Great Haw directly ahead. After a longish climb the
track makes a pronounced swing to the right where
it fords a beck. Here leave it and continue straight
on, using a somewhat damp groove as a guide.

Before long the watershed is met,
marked by a line of fence-posts: ahead are the
hills of Wensleydale. Follow these posts along to
the right, avoiding the soggiest parts and the two

tarns to rise to the highest point of Great Haw, just a little to the right of the posts. On leaving, rejoin the posts to begin the longest, dampest section to the prominent lump of South Haw, a long mile to the south-east. Having enjoyed the view — on this occasion from solid ground — retrace steps the few yards to a gateway in the fence-cum-broken wall to join an inter-valley bridleway. Turn left to trace it's course through the heather, just about discernable by virtue of it's grassy nature. As the descent towards the valley steepens the path may easily be lost, but this matters little as the broad track it eventually joins cannot be missed.

Following the track to the right an old shaft is reached beyond a gate: here branch left to descend to a wide stony track. This leads us to the right, over two small becks to meet a wall. Here take a right fork, the track remaining fairly level through several gates and a short marshy section.

Before long it drops down to join our outgoing path at the end of the dam, from where steps can then be retraced to the car-park.

The extensive quarries on Carle Side were used in the reservoir construction. The track we take up there was originally the tramway used to bring the stone down the fell.

High above the car-park is another quarry with a similar tramway, useful as a viewpoint for those not straying far from their cars.

Dale Edge and Nidderdale from the Stone Man in Woogill

Great Haw is a damp, shapeless mound, but a fine viewpoint. To the west are the fells of Meugher, Great Whernside, Little Whernside, Buckden Pike and Penhill. More distantly is the industrial sprawl of Teeside and the long line of the Cleveland Hills to the east. The highlight in late summer, however, is the glorious sea of purple stretching immediately away to the north and east.

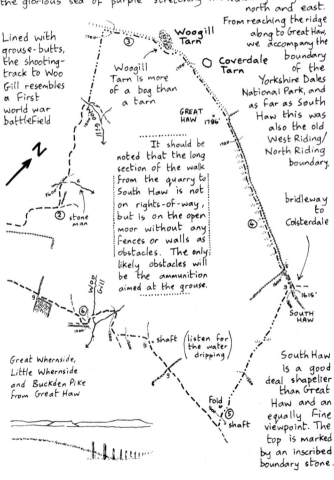

Woogill Tarn

Coverdale Tarn

Lined with grouse-butts, the shooting-track to Woo Gill resembles a First World War battlefield

Woogill Tarn is more of a bog than a tarn

GREAT HAW 1786'

From reaching the ridge along to Great Haw, we accompany the boundary of the Yorkshire Dales National Park, and as far as South Haw this was also the old West Riding/ North Riding boundary.

It should be noted that the long section of the walk from the quarry to South Haw is not on rights-of-way, but is on the open moor without any fences or walls as obstacles. The only likely obstacles will be the ammunition aimed at the grouse.

② stone man

bridleway to Colsterdale

④

1600' 1615' SOUTH HAW

⑥

Woo Gill

1200'

shaft (listen for the water dripping)

Great Whernside, Little Whernside and Buckden Pike from Great Haw

fold ⑤ shaft

South Haw is a good deal shapelier than Great Haw and an equally fine viewpoint. The top is marked by an inscribed boundary stone.

WALK 17

4 miles

from Greenhow

An exploration of bleak upland and old mines

There is limited parking by the main road through the village, but the inn has a good-sized car-park

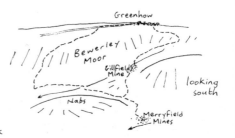

THE WALK

From the Miner's Arms turn right along the road, forsaking it after 100 yards (before reaching the church) for an enclosed track on the right. It takes us down to Far Side, where rounding the corner of the building turn sharp right on an indistinct path which soon improves. Passing the buildings at Low Far Side, our track now drops down through two gateways to enter the environs of Gillfield Mine. The main track threads through the heart of this one-time busy mining scene and on leaving it, takes a left turn at a T-junction of tracks to descend to cross the beck, before rising again across the hillside.

Just level with the scant remains of Near Hardcastle, take the track which joins ours at a right-angle. Almost at once it swings sharp left and becoming enclosed by walls it soon arrives at a gate. Beyond, another wide track is met: from here the short detour to Merryfield Mines can be made. Having returned to (or never having left) this point, follow the track to the right, crossing Brandstone Dub Bridge before continuing to the farm at Hill End.

Ignore the first track to the right after the farm, but cross the bridge and take the one a few yards further, which doubles back rather sharply. Initially a steep pull, remain on the track until a gate bars the way: beyond it a green path rises to the entrance to Coldstonesfold Farm. From here a good track climbs up to a lane rising to the main road opposite Coldstones Quarry. Turn right for the village.

Brief plan of the remains of Gillfield Lead Mine

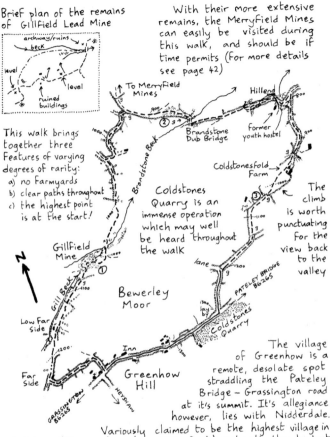

With their more extensive remains, the Merryfield Mines can easily be visited during this walk, and should be if time permits (For more details see page 42)

This walk brings together three features of varying degrees of rarity:
a) no farmyards
b) clear paths throughout
c) the highest point is at the start!

Coldstones Quarry is an immense operation which may well be heard throughout the walk

Bewerley Moor

The climb is worth punctuating for the view back to the valley

The village of Greenhow is a remote, desolate spot straddling the Pateley Bridge - Grassington road at it's summit. It's allegiance however, lies with Nidderdale. Variously claimed to be the highest village in Yorkshire (the road reaches 1320 feet) and with the highest Parish Church — at 1281 feet — in England, Greenhow is certainly exposed. This is no ancient settlement, for it's beginnings stemmed from the lead mines on the nearby moors: evidence of this is everywhere, from the name of the inn to the carving on the roadside war memorial. Much earlier however, were the Romans, who left inscribed pigs of lead as proof of their efforts. Two miles to the west are the famous show-caves, Stump Cross Caverns.

57

WALK 18

7 miles

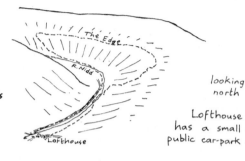

GOYDEN POT AND THE EDGE

from Lofthouse

A fine terrace-walk in the upper valley and a visit to it's two famous pot-holes

looking north

Lofthouse has a small public car-park

THE WALK

Take the Masham road out of Lofthouse which begins to climb immediately past the last houses. Before the first bend however, we leave it along a level track to the left. Beyond a gate this track, known as Thrope Lane, undulates above the River Nidd as it leads us unerringly to Thrope Farm, the first buildings met so far. Remain on the track past the farm to gradually drop down to the river, or at least it's stony course. Continue upstream a short distance to reach Dry Wath, a ford which we use to cross to a gate. A good path continues beyond the gate, following the curves of the river as we cross and recross a fence by stiles. After the second one the path rises to the right to join the drive to Limley Farm.

Head through the farmyard, turning right and then left to pass round the buildings. Behind the last barn a path descends through a thick nettle-field to cross the river-bed to a gate. Beyond it carry on alongside a collapsed wall, past a barn to join a track which zig-zags through trees up the steep hillside. At the top it leads to a gate to enter the now quiet confines of Thwaite House. Take the gateway to the left of the buildings and leave them behind on an enclosed track, which soon emerges into more open country to contour, without difficulty, in a large loop round to the farm of Bracken Ridge.

Behind the gate to the farm, turn right up the access track which itself swings left to begin a long traverse of The Edge. With a wide track the whole way, a wall to the left and steep slopes to the right, we pass by several cottages and farms on the left. Beyond New Houses Edge Farm, the last of these, the track fords a beck past which there is, for the first time, no accompaniment on the left side: just a little further take a track which branches left to descend a field. On reaching a gate near a barn the track heads across fields to approach the river, which it now follows downstream to New Houses Bridge.

Do not cross the shapeley bridge but head along the track into New Houses Farm, turning right after the first building to a small gate. A few yards beyond is a large gate: from it head away alongside the wall to a stile near the river. Follow the Nidd round to a footbridge, crossing it and continuing alongside the river. After a pair of stiles the swallow-hole of Manchester Hole is reached under the cliff of Beggarmoat Scar, and only five minutes further downstream (or 'down-bed' as the case may be) will be located Goyden Pot itself, a stile having to be crossed to gain access.

From Goyden Pot climb the grassy slope on our side of the river to a gate in a fence. Behind it is the water-board road to Scar House Reservoir, and by turning left this road will return us to the toll-booth at it's outset near Lofthouse. Here turn left to a footbridge over the river, but before crossing it, a short detour is recommended. Follow the river upstream, past a wall, and only a few yards further is a dark, wooded dell where a charming waterfall can be found. On returning to cross the bridge, a path to the right leads up into the centre of Lofthouse.

Thwaite House

The Edge (not to be confused with the higher level Dale Edge) is a fine platform along which several farms are based and from where good views of the valley can be had.

Thwaite House was once a grange of Fountains Abbey, but this fine farmstead now stands unoccupied (the only such one on the walk).

Note that opportunities exist to shorten the walk — and to avoid the hilly parts — namely at Thrope Farm and Limley Farm.

Thrope Farm had it's own watermill until the beginning of the century.

Our return route from Goyden Pot makes use of the water-board road serving the dale-head reservoirs. Although maps indicate rights-of-way along the river-bank, they are either difficult or less pleasant to follow. The road is quiet, with grassy verges and is dead level. This last feature is due to the fact that this was the course of the Nidd Valley Light Railway, completed by Bradford Corporation in 1908 to transport equipment to build Angram dam. Passenger services operated from Pateley Bridge as far as Lofthouse, but the line was dismantled after it had also helped with the erection of Scar House dam. Adjacent to (and visible from) Manchester Hole it used a short tunnel, now bricked up.

M = Manchester Hole
G = Goyden Pot

The entrance to Goyden Pot

Goyden Pot and Manchester Hole are well-known names in Upper Nidderdale. The latter is the higher of the two and here is the swallow-hole down which the Nidd quietly departs. When the flow of water is too strong, the river runs on another 300 yards or so to the gaping hole of Goyden Pot. From here the river flows for two miles underground to re-emerge below Lofthouse. Though the main chamber can easily be entered, the inner depths contain a maze of passages which are best left to the well-equipped. If confused by the source of running water in the Limley area, it is likely to be from Limley Gill (see map).

Nidd Falls, Lofthouse

Lofthouse is a small, tidy village, standing above the river with it's houses clinging to the steep road that starts it's journey out of the valley here. This moorland road to Masham is the only exit from the valley above Pateley Bridge, and even this was only made fit for traffic in the 1960's. Now without even it's bus service, the village once had it's own railway station, the highest on the Nidd Valley Light Railway.

The Post Office (a homely place), the Hotel and the village hall are grouped close together, along with an attractive drinking-trough bearing interesting words. Just across the river the water-board road to the head of the valley begins, adjacent to the beautifully-sited cricket pitch. This must be a keen team to make some of the journeys they'll need to!

LOG OF THE WALKS

These two pages provide an opportunity to maintain a permanent record of the walks completed

WALK	DATE	TIME Start	Finish	WEATHER	COMMENTS
1					
2					
3					
4					
5					
6					
7					
8					

| WALK | DATE | TIME | | WEATHER | COMMENTS |
		Start	Finish		
9					
10					
11					
12					
13					
14					
15					
16					
17					
18					

KEY TO THE MAP SYMBOLS

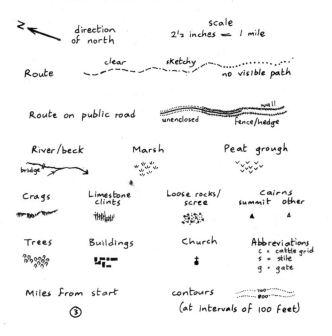

direction of north

scale
2½ inches = 1 mile

Route — clear — sketchy — no visible path

Route on public road — wall — unenclosed — fence/hedge

River/beck — bridge

Marsh

Peat grough

Crags

Limestone clints

Loose rocks/scree

Cairns — summit — other

Trees

Buildings

Church

Abbreviations
c = cattle grid
s = stile
g = gate

Miles from start — ③

contours — 700 — 800 — (at intervals of 100 feet)

THE COUNTRY CODE

Respect the life and work of the countryside
Protect wildlife, plants and trees
Keep to public paths across farmland
Safeguard water supplies
Go carefully on country roads
Keep dogs under control
Guard against all risks of fire
Fasten all gates
Leave no litter – take it with you
Make no unnecessary noise
Leave livestock, crops and machinery alone
Use gates and stiles to cross fences, hedges
and walls